This journal belongs to

....

Footprints Journal

© 2008 Ellie Claire Gift & Paper Corp.
www.ellieclaire.com

Compiled by Barbara Farmer
Designed by Lisa & Jeff Franke

ISBN 978-1-934770-23-8

Printed in China

Footprints
journal

Ellie Claire

gift & paper expressions

...inspired by life

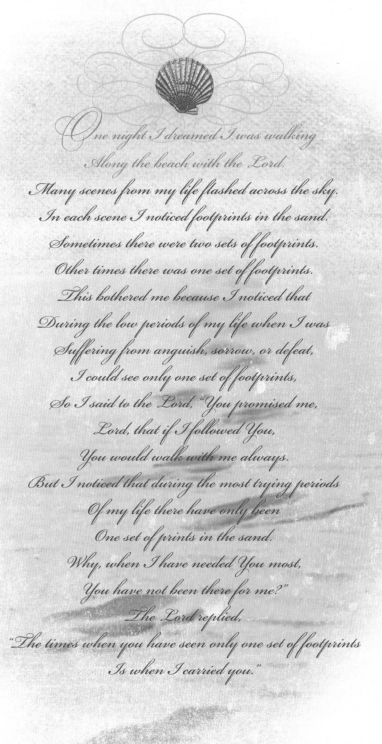

One night I dreamed I was walking
Along the beach with the Lord.
Many scenes from my life flashed across the sky.
In each scene I noticed footprints in the sand.
Sometimes there were two sets of footprints.
Other times there was one set of footprints.
This bothered me because I noticed that
During the low periods of my life when I was
Suffering from anguish, sorrow, or defeat,
I could see only one set of footprints.
So I said to the Lord, "You promised me,
Lord, that if I followed You,
You would walk with me always.
But I noticed that during the most trying periods
Of my life there have only been
One set of prints in the sand.
Why, when I have needed You most,
You have not been there for me?"
The Lord replied,
"The times when you have seen only one set of footprints
Is when I carried you."

*One night I dreamed I was walking
along the beach with the Lord...*

How vital that we pray, armed with the knowledge that God is
in heaven.... Spend some time walking in the workshop of the heavens,
seeing what God has done, and watch how your prayers are energized.

MAX LUCADO

12/31/08

What a way of life! Today I worked all day on the 2009 plan. Girls were out of control as usual. Tammy came home from work about 3 and began her daily drunk. It was ugly. Went to bed about 10:30pm to get away from her mouth. What to do?

1/1/09

Another bizarre day. T was drunk by 7 pm. Falling down, slurring. To bed early.

1/2/09

Worked all day while T & girls went shopping. They came here @ 3pm. She was hammered by 5

1/2 (cont.)

lay 7 she was verbally abusive.
Again, I went to bed to get away
from her. — Hers was a bottle of wine

1/3/09 Slept till 9:30 Aus
went out to Chipotle & errands.
I drank a bottle of champagne
lay 6. I worked till 7 then
ate @ Subway. Built a fire
and she called the fire co.
who came. Lt. said that they
have alot of calls because so may
have fireplaces. She has girls in
our bed and will not let me
in there. I will sleep downstairs

And He walks with me, and He talks with me, and He tells me
I am His own. And the joy we share as we tarry there
none other has ever known.

C. AUSTIN MILES

Love the Lord your God, walk in all His ways, obey His commands, hold firmly to Him, and serve Him with all your heart and all your soul.

JOSHUA 22:5 NLT

1/4/08

Slept downstairs last night. I kept turning up heat during the night — started bad words. I am working in my office today.

1/5/09

Went out & about for awhile today. At Woolfire @ arts lunch then called and picked up T. Watched Ravens game and drank. I blew it. Spent the night out and did not come home until 8 the next day. Anger, resentment.

One night I dreamed I was walking along the beach with the Lord...

1/6/09 Rough day in meeting.
Asked God to help me.
This was one really tough day —
Broken news.

1/7/09 Very full day. Left for Denver
by 1pm. I have been reflecting on
many things... one overriding thought —
I cannot find fault of Sam and the
girls for things that I also am guilty of.
I need to clean up my own back yard.
Focus on my own behavior and
change me — do not demand change
for those people and things around
me — change me!

May your footsteps set you upon a lifetime journey of love. May you wake each day with His blessings and sleep each night in His keeping. And may you always walk in His tender care.

*W*alk in all the way that the Lord your God has commanded you, so that you may live and prosper and prolong your days.

DEUTERONOMY 5:33 NIV

Ate dinner in D. w/ Jerry, Sam, Michael, @ Jax. Early to bed.

1/8/09
Denver. All day meetings w/ groups @ Wynkoop - Brutal! Facts & figures. I really don't feel like I am a part of it all - like an outsider. Why is this? I don't feel good enough. Had a good group dinner.

1/16
Friday night & we took girls to ODY's. Stopped @ Uncle Julios - got smashed. Term started again when we got home. I went to bed.

1/18.
Play off game Balt & Steelers. Went to woodfire. Had fun but Balt. lost

T. started drinking wine and got really
out of hand. She was falling all over
the place. Got home about 10 pm.
Her usual self. Stock her AUNTSX.
1/19.
    I drove to Pittsburgh - 8 hrs.
1/20 Spent day at Mach Heath
then drove to Shirley.
1/21
    Had great day in Shirley of Cheryl &
Vinie. Got home about 7:30. T. drinking
again. Went to bed @ 9pm
1/22
    T. off work.

You're blessed when you stay on course, walking steadily on the road revealed by God. You're blessed when you follow His directions, doing your best to find Him.

PSALM 119:1 THE MESSAGE

1/23.

Friday. I had an appointment w/ Dr. Leicht. Told him what was going on. He advised me to leave and seperate from T. I have not had anything to drink since Sunday.

1/24.

T & I went out to Griffins. All ok until she wanted shots. Again, she got nasty. (I was $270 @ keno. I went to bed early. Thanks!

1/25

Up early. Took a nap. T is drinking again. T. slept it off. Girls are eating cookies @ 3pm. Everything is out of Control. Someone has to take charge. No parent.

*One night I dreamed I was walking
along the beach with the Lord...*

1/28 Kids out of school for day 2 and
well be off tomorrow. T off also due
to weather. ✓ went to Chips for lunch
They went to PF Changs — T came home
w/ a buzz. We drank together after
kids went to bed. It got ugly - T doesn't
get it.✓

1/29
Bad day - T was on a very angry
roll. Mean, talking behind my back
mean things in front of the girls.
I wanted to take a nap but T
would not let me - in & out.
Her day off is always bad.

*The Lord's goodness surrounds us at every moment. I walk
through it almost with difficulty, as through thick grass and flowers.*

R. W. BARBER

He has shown you, O man, what is good. And what does the Lord require of you? To act justly and to love mercy and to walk humbly with your God.

MICAH 6:8 NIV

1/30
Friday night. T took girls to O's. We drank when she got home till the wee hours.

1/31
Uneventful Sat.

1/2 Super Bowl Sunday. T was drunk by game time.

1/4.
I traveled to Boston for the day. Got home about 7:30 T drunk Ashby asked me "what are you drunk ban like now"? when we were playing the wii.

1/5.

Busy day. Had my review w/ Rex and got an A+. Had a few beers and got a bottle of Tosc. In bed by 10.

1/6

Another Friday — T took girls to O's. I let her have it after she got home. I saw Dr. L. today and he feels it is best for me to leave. T. T. does not understand it. I need to be gone by 3/1.

God, my shepherd! I don't need a thing. You have bedded me down in lush
meadows, You find me quiet pools to drink from. True to Your word,
You let me catch my breath and send me in the right direction.

PSALM 23:1-3 THE MESSAGE

2/7

On 2/7/08 Dad died. I miss him.
Today I rode my bike. I drank by
myself. Went to dinner @ Outback.
Home by 9:30 — asleep by 10.
(offered T. a check #1911 for gas.
2/8.   she tore it up)

Up @ 7:30. T. wants to get into it.
Very bitter, argumentative, wants me
to support her ê gets thru school you
here. Decided to ride. went to
Rehobeth Beach — it was a dry clear
gorgeous day! left @ 11 - home by 5:45.
Turns drunk! She said she talked of
ody? I slept a couch.
2/9

T still pissed this morning.

*One night I dreamed I was walking
along the beach with the Lord...*

10/7 Decided to start writing here. Two places?

*All the way to heaven is heaven begun to the Christian who
walks near enough to God to hear the secrets He has to impart.*
E. M. BOUNDS

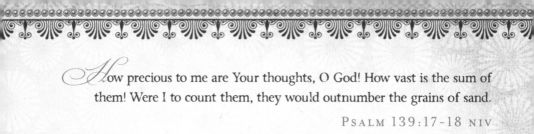

How precious to me are Your thoughts, O God! How vast is the sum of them! Were I to count them, they would outnumber the grains of sand.

PSALM 139:17-18 NIV

One night I dreamed I was walking
Along the beach with the Lord.
Many scenes from my life flashed across the sky.
In each scene I noticed footprints in the sand.
Sometimes there were two sets of footprints.
Other times there was one set of footprints.
This bothered me because I noticed that
During the low periods of my life when I was
Suffering from anguish, sorrow, or defeat,
I could see only one set of footprints.
So I said to the Lord, "You promised me,
Lord, that if I followed You,
You would walk with me always.
But I noticed that during the most trying periods
Of my life there have only been
One set of prints in the sand.
Why, when I have needed You most,
You have not been there for me?"
The Lord replied,
"The times when you have seen only one set of footprints
Is when I carried you."

Many scenes from my life
flashed across the sky...

Although mementos can be preserved or displayed behind glass, memories live on in the heart, where they deepen and resonate over the years, providing strength and comfort in times of need.

*R*emember, O Lord, Your tender mercies and
Your lovingkindnesses, for they are from of old.

PSALM 25:6 NKJV

Many scenes from my life
flashed across the sky...

Memory is history recorded in our brain, memory is a painter,
it paints pictures of the past and of the day.

GRANDMA MOSES

*R*emember the wonders He has performed,
His miracles, and the rulings He has given.

PSALM 105:5 NLT

Many scenes from my life flashed across the sky...

The space between yesterday and today is filled with acceptance, forgiveness and remembering to laugh.

*L*et all who take refuge in You be glad; let them ever sing for joy. Spread Your protection over them, that those who love Your name may rejoice in You.

PSALM 5:11 NIV

Many scenes from my life
flashed across the sky...

---

*O*ne of the great secrets for growing up in Christ is to remember that whether we're riding a bus or working in the office or washing dishes at home or playing a game of golf, Jesus Christ is there.

LEIGHTON FORD

The Lord looks down from heaven upon the children of men,
to see if there are any who understand, who seek God.

PSALM 14:2 NKJV

Many scenes from my life
flashed across the sky...

....

....

....

....

....

....

....

....

....

....

*M*oments spent listening, talking, playing, and sharing together
may be the most important times of all.

GLORIA GAITHER

Dear friends, let us continue to love one another, for love comes from God. Anyone who loves is a child of God and knows God.

1 JOHN 4:7 NLT

Many scenes from my life
flashed across the sky...

You can never change the past. But by the grace of God, you can
win the future. So remember those things which will help you
forward, but forget those things which will only hold you back.

RICHARD C. WOODSOME

I know that I have not yet reached that goal, but there is one thing I always do. Forgetting the past and straining toward what is ahead, I keep trying to reach the goal and get the prize for which God called me.

PHILIPPIANS 3:13-14 NCV

Many scenes from my life
flashed across the sky...

You will find as you look back upon your life, that the moments when you have really lived are the moments when you have done things in the spirit of love.

HENRY DRUMMOND

The fruit of the Spirit is love, joy, peace, patience, kindness, goodness, faithfulness, gentleness and self-control.

GALATIANS 5:22-23 NIV

One night I dreamed I was walking
Along the beach with the Lord.
Many scenes from my life flashed across the sky.
In each scene I noticed footprints in the sand.
Sometimes there were two sets of footprints.
Other times there was one set of footprints.
This bothered me because I noticed that
During the low periods of my life when I was
Suffering from anguish, sorrow, or defeat,
I could see only one set of footprints,
So I said to the Lord, "You promised me,
Lord, that if I followed You,
You would walk with me always.
But I noticed that during the most trying periods
Of my life there have only been
One set of prints in the sand.
Why, when I have needed You most,
You have not been there for me?"
The Lord replied,
"The times when you have seen only one set of footprints
Is when I carried you."

Sometimes there were two sets of footprints...

*Y*our walk with God is essential. His heart is not seen in an
occasional chat or weekly visit. We learn His will as we
take up residence in His house every single day.

MAX LUCADO

hose who know Your name will put their trust in You;
for You, Lord, have not forsaken those who seek You.

PSALM 9:10 NKJV

God came to us because God wanted to join us on the road, to listen to our story, and to help us realize that we are not walking in circles but moving toward the house of peace and joy.

HENRI J. M. NOUWEN

For this God is our God for ever and ever;
He will be our guide even to the end.

PSALM 48:14 NIV

Sometimes there were two sets of footprints...

It is God to whom and with whom we travel, and while He is the End of our journey, He is also at every stopping place.

ELISABETH ELLIOT

Surely goodness and mercy shall follow me all the days of my life;
and I will dwell in the house of the Lord forever.

PSALM 23:6 NKJV

Sometimes there were two sets of footprints...

*Joy is...deeper than an emotional expression of happiness.
Joy is a growing, evolving manifestation of God in my life
as I walk with Him.*

BONNIE MONSON

I will sing for joy in God, explode in praise from deep in my soul!...
For as the earth bursts with spring wildflowers...so the Master, God, brings
righteousness into full bloom and puts praise on display before the nations.

ISAIAH 61:10-11 THE MESSAGE

Sometimes there were two sets of footprints...

They travel lightly whom God's grace carries.
THOMAS À KEMPIS

*A*ccept My teachings and learn from Me, because I am gentle and humble in spirit, and you will find rest for your lives. The burden that I ask you to accept is easy; the load I give you to carry is light.

MATTHEW 11:29-30 NCV

Sometimes there were two sets of footprints...

We walk without fear, full of hope and courage and strength to do His will, waiting for the endless good which He is always giving as fast as He can get us able to take it in.

GEORGE MACDONALD

God can pour on the blessings in astonishing ways so that you're ready for anything and everything, more than just ready to do what needs to be done.

2 CORINTHIANS 9:8 THE MESSAGE

Sometimes there were two sets of footprints...

Faith is meant to be lived moment by moment. It isn't some broad, general outline—it's a long walk with a real Person.

JONI EARECKSON TADA

By entering through faith into what God has always wanted to do for us...
we have it all together with God because of our Master Jesus.... We throw
open our doors to God and discover at the same moment that He has
already thrown open His door to us.

ROMANS 5:1-2 THE MESSAGE

One night I dreamed I was walking
Along the beach with the Lord.
Many scenes from my life flashed across the sky.
In each scene I noticed footprints in the sand.
Sometimes there were two sets of footprints.
Other times there was one set of footprints.

This bothered me because I noticed that
During the low periods of my life when I was
Suffering from anguish, sorrow, or defeat,
I could see only one set of footprints,
So I said to the Lord, "You promised me,
Lord, that if I followed You,
You would walk with me always.
But I noticed that during the most trying periods
Of my life there have only been
One set of prints in the sand.
Why, when I have needed You most,
You have not been there for me?"
The Lord replied,
"The times when you have seen only one set of footprints
Is when I carried you."

Othertimes there was one set of footprints...

We don't walk spiritually by electric light, but by a hand-held
lantern. And a lantern shows only the next step—
not several steps ahead.

AMY CARMICHAEL

*Y*our word is a lamp to my feet and a light to my path.

PSALM 119:105 NKJV

Othertimes there was one set of footprints...

The "air" which our souls need also envelops all of us at all times and on all sides. God is round about us in Christ on every hand, with many-sided and all-sufficient grace. All we need to do is to open our hearts.

OLE HALLESBY

*G*od made my life complete when I placed all the pieces before Him.... God rewrote the text of my life when I opened the book of my heart to His eyes.

PSALM 18:20, 24 THE MESSAGE

Othertimes there was one set of footprints...

When you take the first step to embrace God in your circumstances,
He will go the distance to embrace you.

STORMIE OMARTIAN

And so, my children, listen to me, for all who follow my ways are joyful....
Joyful are those who listen to me, watching for me daily at my gates....
For whoever finds me finds life and receives favor from the Lord.

PROVERBS 8:32-35 NLT

Othertimes there was one set of footprints...

If God chooses not to fill us, He has something to say through our emptiness. The only ones who ever come up full are the ones who are willing to be presented empty.

JOHN FISHER

He satisfies the thirsty and fills the hungry with good things.... He led them from the darkness and deepest gloom; He snapped their chains. Let them praise the Lord...for the wonderful things He has done for them.

PSALM 107:9, 14-15 NLT

Othertimes there was one set of footprints...

You are never alone. In your heart of hearts, in the place where no two people are ever alike, Christ is waiting for you. And what you never dared hope for springs to life.

ROGER OF TAIZÉ

You have this faith and love because of your hope, and what you hope for is kept safe for you in heaven.

COLOSSIANS 1:5 NCV

Othertimes there was one set of footprints...

He who has God and everything has no more than he who has God alone.

C. S. LEWIS

My soul finds rest in God alone; my salvation comes from Him.

PSALM 62:1 NIV

Othertimes there was one set of footprints...

We are not alone on our journey. The God of love who gave us life sent us [His] only Son to be with us at all times and in all places, so that we never have to feel lost in our struggles but always can trust that God walks with us.

HENRI J. M. NOUWEN

God loved the world so much that He gave His one and only Son so that whoever believes in Him may not be lost, but have eternal life. God did not send His Son into the world to judge the world guilty, but to save the world through Him.

JOHN 3:16-17 NCV

One night I dreamed I was walking
Along the beach with the Lord.
Many scenes from my life flashed across the sky.
In each scene I noticed footprints in the sand.
Sometimes there were two sets of footprints.
Other times there was one set of footprints.
This bothered me because I noticed that
During the low periods of my life when I was
Suffering from anguish, sorrow, or defeat,
I could see only one set of footprints.
So I said to the Lord, "You promised me,
Lord, that if I followed You,
You would walk with me always.
But I noticed that during the most trying periods
Of my life there have only been
One set of prints in the sand.
Why, when I have needed You most,
You have not been there for me?"
The Lord replied,
"The times when you have seen only one set of footprints
Is when I carried you."

During the low periods of my life...

I could see only one set of footprints...

....

....

....

....

....

....

....

....

....

....

....

....

....

What matters supremely is not the fact that I know God, but the larger fact...that *He knows me*.... I am never out of His mind. All my knowledge of Him depends on His sustained initiative in knowing me.

J. I. PACKER

I will give you the wealth that is stored away and the hidden riches so you will know I am the Lord, the God of Israel, who calls you by name.

ISAIAH 45:3 NCV

During the low periods of my life...
I could see only one set of footprints...

Nothing enters your life accidently—remember that. Behind our every experience is our loving, sovereign God.

*T*o everything there is a season, a time for every purpose under heaven.

ECCLESIASTES 3:1 NKJV

During the low periods of my life...
I could see only one set of footprints...

When I walk by the wayside, He is along with me.... Amid all my forgetfulness of Him, He never forgets me.

THOMAS CHALMERS

And I am convinced that nothing can ever separate us from God's love. Neither death nor life…, neither our fears for today nor our worries about tomorrow—not even the powers of hell can separate us from God's love.

ROMANS 8:38 NLT

During the low periods of my life...
I could see only one set of footprints...

God walks with us.... He scoops us up in His arms or simply sits with us in silent strength until we cannot avoid the awesome recognition that yes, even now, He is here.

GLORIA GAITHER

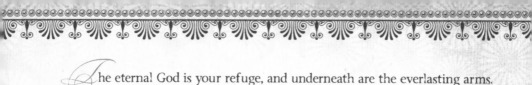

*T*he eternal God is your refuge, and underneath are the everlasting arms.

DEUTERONOMY 33:27 NKJV

During the low periods of my life...
I could see only one set of footprints...

What is the Lord saying? There's only one message: "Trust Me.
Even when you don't understand and can't comprehend: trust Me!"

JAMES DOBSON

Blessed are those who trust in the Lord and have made the Lord their hope and confidence.

JEREMIAH 17:7 NLT

During the low periods of my life...
I could see only one set of footprints...

_know not where His islands lift their fronded palms in air;
I only know I cannot drift beyond His love and care.

JOHN GREENLEAF WHITTIER

I pray that you and all God's holy people will have the power to understand the greatness of Christ's love—how wide and how long and how high and how deep that love is.

EPHESIANS 3:18 NCV

During the low periods of my life...
I could see only one set of footprints...

here is no need to plead that the love of God shall fill our hearts as though He were unwilling to fill us.... Love is pressing around us on all sides like air. Cease to resist it and instantly love takes possession.

AMY CARMICHAEL

Christ's love is greater than anyone can ever know, but I pray that you will be able to know that love. Then you can be filled with the fullness of God.

EPHESIANS 3:19 NCV

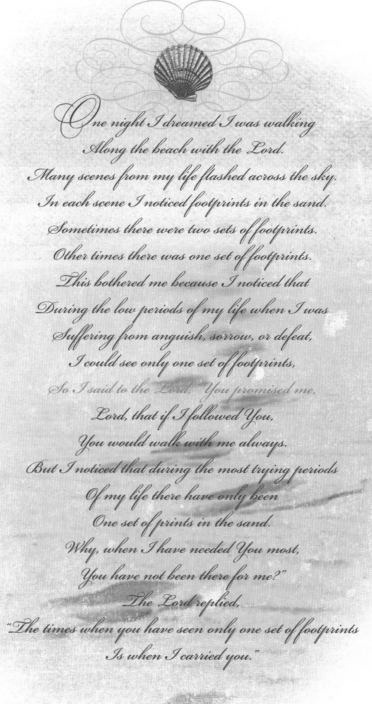

One night I dreamed I was walking
Along the beach with the Lord.
Many scenes from my life flashed across the sky.
In each scene I noticed footprints in the sand.
Sometimes there were two sets of footprints.
Other times there was one set of footprints.
This bothered me because I noticed that
During the low periods of my life when I was
Suffering from anguish, sorrow, or defeat,
I could see only one set of footprints,
So I said to the Lord, "You promised me,
Lord, that if I followed You,
You would walk with me always.
But I noticed that during the most trying periods
Of my life there have only been
One set of prints in the sand.
Why, when I have needed You most,
You have not been there for me?"
The Lord replied,
"The times when you have seen only one set of footprints
Is when I carried you."

So I said to the Lord, "You promised me..."

Be assured, if you walk with Him and look to Him and expect help from Him, He will never fail you.

GEORGE MUELLER

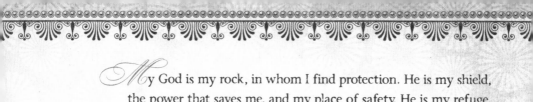

My God is my rock, in whom I find protection. He is my shield, the power that saves me, and my place of safety. He is my refuge.

2 SAMUEL 22:3 NLT

So I said to the Lord, "You promised me..."

The hope we have in Christ is an absolute certainty....
Everything He promised He will deliver.

BILLY GRAHAM

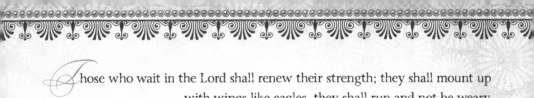

*T*hose who wait in the Lord shall renew their strength; they shall mount up with wings like eagles, they shall run and not be weary, they shall walk and not faint.

ISAIAH 40:31 NKJV

So I said to the Lord, "You promised me..."

We cannot see the way God is going to work where we are right now, but be sure, He will.

JACK HAYFORD

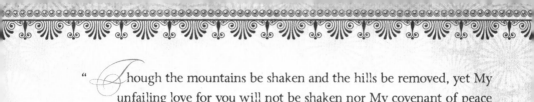

"Though the mountains be shaken and the hills be removed, yet My unfailing love for you will not be shaken nor My covenant of peace be removed," says the Lord, who has compassion on you.

ISAIAH 54:10 NIV

So I said to the Lord, "You promised me..."

*Remember you are very special to God.... He has promised to
complete the good work He has begun in you. As you continue to grow
in Him, He will teach you to be a blessing to others.*

GARY SMALLEY AND JOHN TRENT

Because you have these blessings, do your best to add these things to your lives: to your faith, add goodness; and to your goodness, add knowledge.

2 PETER 1:5 NCV

So I said to the Lord, "You promised me..."

Tarry at the promise till God meets you there. He always returns by way of His promises.

L. B. COWMAN

*G*od's way is perfect. All the Lord's promises prove true. He is a shield for all who look to Him for protection.

PSALM 18:30 NLT

So I said to the Lord, "You promised me..."

If God, like a father, denies us what we want now, it is in order to give us some far better thing later on. The will of God, we can rest assured, is invariably a better thing.

ELISABETH ELLIOT

*E*ven though you are bad, you know how to give good gifts to your children. How much more your heavenly Father will give good things to those who ask Him!

MATTHEW 7:11 NCV

So I said to the Lord, "You promised me..."

We may...depend upon God's promises, for...He will be as good as His word. He is so kind that He cannot deceive us, so true that He cannot break His promise.

MATTHEW HENRY

The Lord is not slow in doing what He promised—the way some people understand slowness. But God is being patient with you. He does not want anyone to be lost, but He wants all people to change their hearts and lives.

2 PETER 3:9 NCV

One night I dreamed I was walking
Along the beach with the Lord.
Many scenes from my life flashed across the sky.
In each scene I noticed footprints in the sand.
Sometimes there were two sets of footprints.
Other times there was one set of footprints.
This bothered me because I noticed that
During the low periods of my life when I was
Suffering from anguish, sorrow, or defeat,
I could see only one set of footprints,
So I said to the Lord, "You promised me,
Lord, that if I followed You,
You would walk with me always.
But I noticed that during the most trying periods
Of my life there have only been
One set of prints in the sand.
Why, when I have needed You most,
You have not been there for me?"
The Lord replied,
"The times when you have seen only one set of footprints
Is when I carried you."

Lord...if I followed You...

When you come looking for Me, you'll find Me. Yes, when you get serious about finding Me and want it more than anything else, I'll make sure you won't be disappointed.

JEREMIAH 29:13 THE MESSAGE

Lord...if I followed You...

Faith, in the Old Testament, is defined by a person's willingness to wait for the promises of God to come. Faith, in the New Testament, means following the Promised One.

MICHAEL CARD

For he who comes to God must believe that He is, and that He is a rewarder of those who diligently seek Him.

HEBREWS 11:6 NKJV

Lord...if I followed You...

As we follow Him who is everlasting we will touch the things that last forever.

From eternity to eternity I am God. No one can snatch anyone out of
My hand. No one can undo what I have done.

ISAIAH 43:13 NLT

Lord...if I followed You...

God did not tell us to follow Him because He needed our help, but because He knew that loving Him would make us whole.

IRENAEUS

I will instruct you and teach you in the way you should go;
I will counsel you and watch over you.

PSALM 32:8 NIV

Lord...if I followed You...

So faith bounds forward to its goal in God, and love can trust her
Lord to lead her there; upheld by Him my soul is following hard,
till God hath full fulfilled my deepest prayer.

F. BROOK

The faithful love of the Lord never ends! His mercies never cease.
Great is His faithfulness; His mercies begin afresh each morning.

LAMENTATIONS 3:22-23 NLT

Lord...if I followed You...

I don't know what the future holds, but I know
who holds the future.

E. STANLEY JONES

"For I know the plans I have for you," declares the Lord, "plans to prosper you and not to harm you, plans to give you hope and a future."

JEREMIAH 29:11 NIV

Lord...if I followed You...

Do you have a place of shelter where you seek only His face? Do you spend time in that secret place? Have you given prayer the priority it deserves? When you pray, remember it is the Lord's face you seek.

CHARLES R. SWINDOLL

He who dwells in the shelter of the Most High
will rest in the shadow of the Almighty.

PSALM 91:1 NIV

One night I dreamed I was walking
Along the beach with the Lord.
Many scenes from my life flashed across the sky.
In each scene I noticed footprints in the sand.
Sometimes there were two sets of footprints.
Other times there was one set of footprints.
This bothered me because I noticed that
During the low periods of my life when I was
Suffering from anguish, sorrow, or defeat,
I could see only one set of footprints,
So I said to the Lord, "You promised me,
Lord, that if I followed You,
You would walk with me always.
But I noticed that during the most trying periods
Of my life there have only been
One set of prints in the sand.
Why, when I have needed You most,
You have not been there for me?"
The Lord replied,
"The times when you have seen only one set of footprints
Is when I carried you."

You would walk with me always...

*J*esus wants to live His life in you, to look through your eyes, walk with your feet, love with your heart.

MOTHER TERESA

I give you a new command: Love each other. You must love each other as I have loved you. All people will know that you are My followers if you love each other.

JOHN 13:34-35 NCV

You would walk with me always...

We are always in the presence of God.... There is never a nonsacred moment! His presence never diminishes. Our awareness of His presence may falter, but the reality of His presence never changes.

MAX LUCADO

I will declare that Your love stands firm forever,
that You established Your faithfulness in heaven itself.

PSALM 89:2 NIV

You would walk with me always...

The crucified Christ is the One who comes to walk with us every day.

ANDREW MURRAY

I am continually with You; You hold me by my right hand. You will guide me with Your counsel, and afterward receive me to glory.

PSALM 73:23-24 NKJV

You would walk with me always...

Look back from where we have come.... How could we know the joy without the suffering? And how could we endure the suffering but that we are warmed and carried on the breast of God?

DESMOND M. TUTU

He comforts us in all our troubles so that we can comfort others....
For the more we suffer for Christ, the more God will shower us
with His comfort through Christ.

2 CORINTHIANS 1:4-5 NLT

You would walk with me always...

God is the sunshine that warms us, the rain that melts the frost and waters the young plants. The presence of God is a climate of strong and bracing love, always there.

JOAN ARNOLD

Therefore know that the Lord your God, He is God, the faithful God who keeps covenant and mercy for a thousand generations with those who love Him and keep His commandments.

DEUTERONOMY 7:9 NKJV

You would walk with me always...

God's hand is always there; once you grasp it you'll never want to let it go.

*L*et us hold firmly to the hope that we have confessed, because we can trust God to do what He promised.

HEBREWS 10:23 NCV

You would walk with me always…

The Lord doesn't always remove the sources of stress in our lives…but He's always there and cares for us. We can feel His arms around us on the darkest night.

JAMES DOBSON

I am with you always, even to the end of the age.

MATTHEW 28:20 NKJV

One night I dreamed I was walking
Along the beach with the Lord.
Many scenes from my life flashed across the sky.
In each scene I noticed footprints in the sand.
Sometimes there were two sets of footprints.
Other times there was one set of footprints.
This bothered me because I noticed that
During the low periods of my life when I was
Suffering from anguish, sorrow, or defeat,
I could see only one set of footprints,
So I said to the Lord, "You promised me,
Lord, that if I followed You,
You would walk with me always.
But I noticed that during the most trying periods
Of my life there have only been
One set of prints in the sand.
Why, when I have needed You most,
You have not been there for me?"
The Lord replied,
"The times when you have seen only one set of footprints
Is when I carried you."

Why, when I have needed You most...

here is a silence into which the world cannot intrude.
There is a peace you carry in your heart and cannot lose.

All who listen to Me will live in peace, untroubled by fear of harm.

PROVERBS 1:33 NLT

Why, when I have needed You most...

When we are in a situation where Jesus is all we have, we soon discover He is all we really need.

GIGI GRAHAM TCHIVIDJIAN

This I declare about the Lord: He alone is my refuge, my place of safety;
He is my God, and I trust Him.

PSALM 91:2 NLT

Why, when I have needed You most...

You can trust God right now to supply all your needs for today.
And if your needs are more tomorrow, His supply will be greater also.

My God shall supply all your need according to His riches
in glory by Christ Jesus.

PHILIPPIANS 4:19 NKJV

Why, when I have needed You most...

Should we feel at times disheartened..., a simple movement of heart toward God will renew our powers. Whatever He may demand of us, He will give us at the moment the strength and courage that we need.

FRANÇOIS FÉNELON

God is my strength, God is my song, and, Yes! God is my salvation.

EXODUS 15:2 THE MESSAGE

Why, when I have needed You most...

God takes care of His own. He knows our needs.... He stands ready to come to our rescue. And at just the right moment He steps in and proves Himself as our faithful heavenly Father.

CHARLES R. SWINDOLL

The Lord your God is with you, He is mighty to save. He will take great delight in you, He will quiet you with His love, He will rejoice over you with singing.

ZEPHANIAH 3:17 NIV

Why, when I have needed You most...

What is important is that you are holding on, that you have got a
grip on Christ and He will not let your hand go.

MOTHER TERESA

I pray that the God who gives hope will fill you with much joy and peace while you trust in Him. Then your hope will overflow by the power of the Holy Spirit.

ROMANS 15:13 NCV

Why, when I have needed You most...

When times get hard, remember Jesus.... When tears come, remember Jesus.... When fear pitches his tent in your front yard. When death looms, when anger singes, when shame weighs heavily. Remember Jesus.

MAX LUCADO

*L*et us fix our eyes on Jesus...who for the joy set before Him endured the cross...and sat down at the right hand of the throne of God...so that you will not grow weary and lose heart.

HEBREWS 12:2-3 NIV

One night I dreamed I was walking
Along the beach with the Lord.
Many scenes from my life flashed across the sky.
In each scene I noticed footprints in the sand.
Sometimes there were two sets of footprints.
Other times there was one set of footprints.
This bothered me because I noticed that
During the low periods of my life when I was
Suffering from anguish, sorrow, or defeat,
I could see only one set of footprints,
So I said to the Lord, "You promised me,
Lord, that if I followed You,
You would walk with me always.
But I noticed that during the most trying periods
Of my life there have only been
One set of prints in the sand.
Why, when I have needed You most,
You have not been there for me?"
The Lord replied,
"The times when you have seen only one set of footprints
Is when I carried you."

Have You not been there for me?...

The great thing to remember is that, though our feelings come and go, His love for us does not.

C. S. LEWIS

We love each other because He loved us first.

1 JOHN 4:19 NLT

Have You not been there for me?...

God never abandons anyone on whom He has set His love; nor does Christ, the good shepherd, ever lose track of His sheep.

J. I. PACKER

I am the good shepherd. The good shepherd gives His life for the sheep.

JOHN 10:11 NCV

Have You not been there for me?...

In those times I can't seem to find God, I rest in the assurance He knows how to find me.

NEVA COYLE

The Lord is with you while you are with Him.
If you seek Him, He will be found by you.

2 CHRONICLES 15:2 NKJV

Have You not been there for me?...

God is waiting for us to come to Him with our needs.... God's throne room is always open.... Every single believer in the whole world could walk into the throne room all at one time, and it would not even be crowded.

CHARLES STANLEY

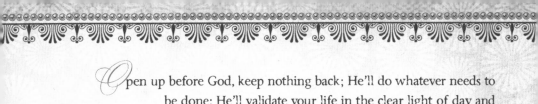

Open up before God, keep nothing back; He'll do whatever needs to be done: He'll validate your life in the clear light of day and stamp you with approval at high noon.

PSALM 37:5 THE MESSAGE

Have You not been there for me?...

The more we depend on God the more dependable we find He is.

CLIFF RICHARD

The Lord will always lead you. He will satisfy your needs in dry lands and give strength to your bones. You will be like a garden that has much water, like a spring that never runs dry.

ISAIAH 58:11 NCV

Have You not been there for me?...

Have confidence in God's mercy, for when you think He is a long way from you, He is often quite near.

THOMAS À KEMPIS

We're depending on God; He's everything we need. What's more, our hearts brim with joy since we've taken for our own His holy name.

PSALM 33:20 THE MESSAGE

Have You not been there for me?...

God has put into each of our lives a void that cannot be filled by the world. We may leave God or put Him on hold, but He is always there, patiently waiting for us...to turn back to Him.

EMILIE BARNES

Behold, I stand at the door and knock. If anyone hears My voice and opens the door, I will come in to him and dine with him, and he with Me.

REVELATION 3:20 NKJV

One night I dreamed I was walking
Along the beach with the Lord.
Many scenes from my life flashed across the sky.
In each scene I noticed footprints in the sand.
Sometimes there were two sets of footprints.
Other times there was one set of footprints.

This bothered me because I noticed that
During the low periods of my life when I was
Suffering from anguish, sorrow, or defeat,
I could see only one set of footprints,
So I said to the Lord, "You promised me,
Lord, that if I followed You,
You would walk with me always.
But I noticed that during the most trying periods
Of my life there have only been
One set of prints in the sand.
Why, when I have needed You most,
You have not been there for me?"

The Lord replied,
"The times when you have seen only one set of footprints
Is when I carried you."

The Lord replied...

Be sure to remember that nothing in your daily life is so insignificant and so inconsequential that God will not help you by answering your prayer.

OLE HALLESBY

I call on you, O God, for you will answer me;
give ear to me and hear my prayer.

PSALM 17:6 NIV

The Lord replied...

Do you know why the mighty God of the universe chooses to answer prayer? It is because His children ask. God delights in our asking. He is pleased at our asking. His heart is warmed by our asking.

RICHARD J. FOSTER

Ask and you'll get; seek and you'll find; knock and the door will open. Don't bargain with God. Be direct. Ask for what you need.

LUKE 11:9 THE MESSAGE

The Lord replied...

God hears and answers;...His ear is ever open to
the cry of His children.

E. M. BOUNDS

I will answer them before they even call to Me. While they are still talking about their needs, I will go ahead and answer their prayers!

ISAIAH 65:24 NLT

The Lord replied...

So wait before the Lord. Wait in the stillness. And in that stillness, assurance will come to you. You will know that you are heard;...you will hear words spoken to you, perhaps to your grateful surprise and refreshment.

AMY CARMICHAEL

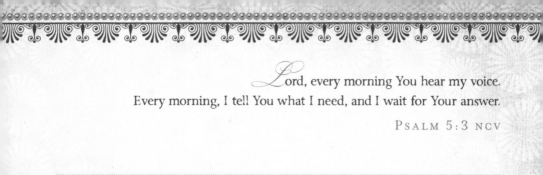

*L*ord, every morning You hear my voice.
Every morning, I tell You what I need, and I wait for Your answer.

PSALM 5:3 NCV

The Lord replied...

What God gives in answer to our prayers will always be the thing we most urgently need, and it will always be sufficient.

ELISABETH ELLIOT

This is your Father you are dealing with, and He knows better than you what you need. With a God like this loving you, you can pray very simply.

MATTHEW 6:7 THE MESSAGE

The Lord replied...

Be patient. Our prayers are always answered, but not always on the exact day we'd like them to be.

MARJORIE TURNER

It is good that one should hope and wait quietly for the salvation of the Lord.

LAMENTATIONS 3:26 NKJV

The Lord replied...

_____

_____

_____

_____

_____

_____

_____

_____

_____

_____

_____

_____

If you find yourself in this spiritual state feeling wayward,
unstable in heart, confused...cling to the Lord in prayer!
He always hears, and He will answer.

TERESA OF AVILA

Then you will call, and the Lord will answer; you will cry
for help, and He will say: Here am I.

ISAIAH 58:9 NIV

One night I dreamed I was walking
Along the beach with the Lord.
Many scenes from my life flashed across the sky.
In each scene I noticed footprints in the sand.
Sometimes there were two sets of footprints.
Other times there was one set of footprints.
This bothered me because I noticed that
During the low periods of my life when I was
Suffering from anguish, sorrow, or defeat,
I could see only one set of footprints,
So I said to the Lord, "You promised me,
Lord, that if I followed You,
You would walk with me always.
But I noticed that during the most trying periods
Of my life there have only been
One set of prints in the sand.
Why, when I have needed You most,
You have not been there for me?"
The Lord replied,
"The times when you have seen only one set of footprints
Is when I carried you."

"The times when you have seen only one set of footprints is when I carried you."

You are in the Beloved...therefore infinitely dear to the Father, unspeakably precious to Him. You are never, not for one second, alone.

NORMAN DOWTY

*L*et the beloved of the Lord rest secure in Him, for He shields him all day
long, and the one the Lord loves rests between His shoulders.

DEUTERONOMY 33:12 NIV

"The times when you have seen only one set of footprints is when I carried you."

God will find us, bless us, even when we feel most alone, unsure.... God will find a way to let us know that He is with us *in this place*, wherever we are.

KATHLEEN NORRIS

You're blessed when you feel you've lost what is most dear to you.
Only then can you be embraced by the One most dear to you.

MATTHEW 5:4 THE MESSAGE

"The times when you have seen only one set of footprints is when I carried you."

With God our trust can be abandoned, utterly free. In Him are no limitations, no flaws, no weaknesses. His judgment is perfect, His knowledge of us is perfect, His love is perfect. God alone is trustworthy.

EUGENIA PRICE

He is like a rock; what He does is perfect, and He is always fair.
He is a faithful God who does no wrong, who is right and fair.

DEUTERONOMY 32:4 NCV

"The times when you have seen only one set of footprints is when I carried you."

Lift up your eyes. Your heavenly Father waits to bless you—
in inconceivable ways to make your life what you
never dreamed it could be.

ANNE ORTLUND

I'm still in Your presence, but You've taken my hand.
You wisely and tenderly lead me, and then You bless me.

PSALM 73:21 THE MESSAGE

"The times when you have seen only one set of footprints is when I carried you."

God guides us.... He leads us step by step.... Only afterwards, as we look back over the way we have come and reconsider certain important moments... do we experience the feeling...that God has mysteriously guided us.

PAUL TOURNIER